Also by

ew Tekulsky

Gourmet Chocolate Drinks

wn Gourmet Tea Drinks

ur Own Ice Pops

n Gourmet Coffee Drinks

mingbird Garden

tterfly Garden

10/97

Math

MAKING YOUR OWN GOURMET SOFT DRINKS

Sodas, Punches, Smoothies, Slushes, and More!

MATHEW TEKULSKY

Illustrations by
Clair Moritz-Magnesio

Crown Publishers, Inc.
New York

Copyright © 1997 by Mathew Tekulsky
Illustrations copyright © 1997 by Clair Moritz-Magnesio

Published by Crown Publishers, Inc.,
201 East 50th Street, New York, New York 10022.
Member of the Crown Publishing Group.

Random House, Inc. New York, Toronto, London, Sydney, Auckland
http://www.randomhouse.com/

CROWN and colophon are trademarks of Crown Publishers, Inc.

Printed in the United States of America

Design by Nancy Kenmore

Library of Congress Cataloging-in-Publication Data
is available upon request.

ISBN 0-517-70831-0

10   9   8   7   6   5   4   3   2   1

First Edition

To my father,
Joseph D. Tekulsky—
to whom I owe everything.

Acknowledgments

Thanks, as always, to all of the great people at Crown Publishers, especially Chip Gibson and Steve Ross. I owe you all a debt of gratitude for allowing me to continue to express myself through my books. Thanks, as always, to my literary agent, Jane Jordan Browne, and to my editor, Brandt Aymar, for their continued support.

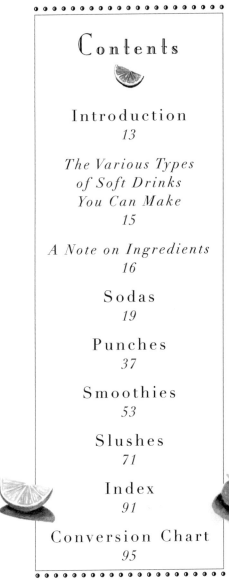

Contents

MAKING YOUR OWN GOURMET SOFT DRINKS

Introduction

You are sitting by the ocean on a Caribbean island. A calm breeze is blowing through your hair as you take another sip of your cool, refreshing drink. • Maybe it is a Kiwi Soda, or a Pineapple-Orange Punch, or a Strawberry-Banana Smoothie, or a Vanilla-Hazelnut Slush. • A tropical bird chirps in the distance, and the sound of the waves is soothing to your ears. • You take another sip of your drink — maybe it is a Cherry-Papaya Slush — and the icy liquid

chills your throat and pleases your palate. • "Ah!" you think. "This is living." • Well, you may not be able to go to a Caribbean island anytime you want, but you can bring the delicious taste of such a paradise to your mouth whenever you please by using the recipes in this book. • There are sodas, punches, smoothies, and slushes from which to *choose — with flavors ranging from citrus (orange, grapefruit, lemon) to berries (strawberry, raspberry, blueberry) to tropical fruits (banana, coconut, papaya).* ◦ *There are colas; flavored syrups such as vanilla, hazelnut, and almond; and there is even a Peanut Smoothie!* ◦ *There are drinks for just about any occasion: a Strawberry Ice Cream Soda for an afternoon party; a Peach-Papaya-Pineapple Punch for a soiree; an Apple Blueberry-Banana Smoothie for a meal in itself; or a Raspberry-Orange Slush as a poolside refresher.* ◦ *Whichever of these soft drinks you decide to make, you are sure to be met with some great taste sensations, a lot of healthful food value, and a convenient and inexpensive way to quench your thirst.* ◦ *Enjoy!*

The Various Types of Soft Drinks You Can Make

SODAS   These are carbonated drinks that are made with either carbonated water or a commercially available soda, such as cola or root beer. The sodas in this book are lightly flavored with fruit juices and are intended to be consumed by one or two people.

PUNCHES   These drinks are more heavily flavored with fruit juices than sodas; they use less carbonated water or commercially available sodas, and sometimes do not use any carbonated beverage at all. The punches in this book are intended to be consumed by four or six people. (I suggest serving punches in individual glasses over ice, but feel free to serve punches in a punch bowl with ice cubes or an ice block, or chill the punch in the refrigerator before serving it and do not use any ice at all. It is up to you.)

SMOOTHIES   These are blended drinks that use fruit juices and milk, frozen and fresh fruit, ice cream or sherbet, and small amounts of crushed ice when necessary to cool a drink down when fresh or thawed fruit such as bananas are used. They are intended to be consumed by one or two people.

SLUSHES   These are blended drinks that use fruit juices and milk, fresh fruit, ice cream or sherbet, and larger amounts of crushed ice resulting in a slushy beverage. They are intended to be consumed by one or two people.

A Note on Ingredients

1. I use regular granulated sugar, but an equal amount of honey can be used as well.

2. I use low-fat milk, but nonfat milk can also be used, depending on your taste.

3. It is always best to use fresh whipped cream — generally about ¼ cup per drink.

4. I use unsweetened cranberry juice and unsweetened cherry juice, which are available at most health food stores.

5. I use bottled or canned fruit nectars, which contain corn syrup. This will make the drink sweeter than if you use unsweetened fruit nectars from freshly juiced fruits.

6. I use Concord grape juice, but feel free to use white grape juice, depending on your taste.

7. I use low-fat yogurt, but nonfat yogurt can also be used.

8. I use ice cream, but feel free to use frozen yogurt, depending on your taste.

9. When used as garnishes, orange, lemon, lime, apple, peach, and grapefruit slices may be peeled or not. It is up to you. Kiwifruit, pineapple, papaya, mango, and banana slices should be peeled.

10. I use canned mandarin orange segments.

11. I use commercially available lemonade that is packaged in cartons, but feel free to use frozen concentrate or make your own lemonade from scratch, depending on your taste.

12. I use flavored gourmet syrups that are commercially available at many coffee shops and gourmet food stores.

13. Unless otherwise stated, I use fresh fruit or thawed frozen fruit. Feel free to use packaged frozen fruit or freeze your own fresh fruit for later use.

14. If you wish to make more (or fewer) servings of these drinks, simply multiply (or divide) the amount of each ingredient to provide for the number of servings that you wish to make.

17
o

SODAS

Orange Soda

This delightful soda is popular all over the world — and for good reason.

½ cup orange juice
   Ice cubes
¾ cup carbonated water

Orange slice, for
garnish

Pour the juice over ice in a tall glass. Stir the carbonated water into the juice and garnish with a slice of orange.

Serves 1

Variation: For a Tangerine Soda, substitute ½ cup tangerine juice for the orange juice and proceed as directed above. Garnish with a segment of tangerine.

Kiwi Soda

Bring the taste of Australia to your palate with this drink.

2 tablespoons kiwi syrup
Ice cubes
1 cup carbonated water
2 tablespoons half-and-
half (optional)

Whipped cream
(optional)
Kiwifruit slices, for
garnish (optional)

Pour the syrup over ice in a tall glass. Add the carbonated water and top with the half-and-half and/or the whipped cream and/or slices of kiwifruit, if desired.

Serves 1

Variations: For a Raspberry Soda, substitute 2 tablespoons raspberry syrup for the kiwi syrup and proceed as directed above. Garnish with fresh raspberries.

For a Strawberry Soda, substitute 2 tablespoons strawberry syrup for the kiwi syrup and proceed as directed above. Garnish with slices of fresh strawberries.

Apricot Soda

The lemon-lime soda sweetens this drink.

½ cup apricot nectar   *½ cup lemon-lime soda*
   Ice cubes

Pour the nectar over ice in a tall glass. Stir the soda into the nectar.

Serves 1

Variation: Substitute ½ cup carbonated water for the lemon-lime soda and proceed as directed above.

Papaya-Grape Soda

The grape juice tastes just as good with the papaya nectar as it does with the mango nectar.

1 cup papaya nectar	*Ice cubes*
½ cup grape juice	*Papaya slices, for*
1 cup carbonated water	*garnish (optional)*

Mix the nectar, juice, and carbonated water together and pour over ice in 2 tall glasses. Garnish with slices of papaya, if desired.

Serves 2

Variation: For a Mango-Grape Soda, substitute 1 cup mango nectar for the papaya nectar and proceed as directed above. Garnish with slices of mango, if desired.

Mango-Orange Soda

This drink makes you feel as if you are on a tropical island.

1 cup mango nectar	Ice cubes
½ cup orange juice	Orange slices, for
1 cup carbonated water	garnish

Mix the nectar, juice, and carbonated water together and pour over ice in 2 tall glasses. Garnish with slices of orange.

Serves 2

Variations: For a Mango-Lemon Soda, substitute 1 teaspoon lemon juice for the orange juice and proceed as directed above. Garnish with slices of lemon.

For a Mango-Lime Soda, substitute 1 teaspoon lime juice for the orange juice and proceed as directed above. Garnish with slices of lime.

Cranberry-Orange Soda

The delicious taste of the cranberry juice combines well with the orange juice in this drink.

¼ cup cranberry juice
¾ cup orange juice
1 cup carbonated water
Ice cubes

Sugar to taste
(optional)
Orange slices, for
garnish

Mix the juices and the carbonated water together and pour over ice in 2 tall glasses. Add sugar, if desired, and garnish with slices of orange.

Serves 2

Variations: For a Cranberry-Apple Soda, substitute ¾ cup apple juice for the orange juice and proceed as directed above.

For a Cranberry-Grape Soda, substitute ¾ cup grape juice for the orange juice and proceed as directed above.

For a Cranberry-Cherry Soda, substitute ¾ cup cherry juice for the orange juice and proceed as directed above.

For a Cranberry-Grapefruit Soda, substitute ¾ cup grapefruit juice for the orange juice and proceed as directed above.

Cranberry — Lemon-Lime Soda

The cranberry juice adds just the right zest to your lemon-lime soda.

    ½ cup cranberry juice   Ice cubes
    1½ cups lemon-lime soda

Mix the juice and the soda together and pour over ice in 2 tall glasses.

Serves 2

Root Beer — Lime Soda

Add the great taste of lime to your root beer with this drink.

    1 cup root beer   ½ teaspoon lime juice
    Ice cubes

Pour the root beer over ice in a tall glass. Stir the juice into the root beer.

Serves 1

Variation: For a Lime Cream Soda, substitute 1 cup cream soda for the root beer and proceed as directed above.

Ginger-Lemon Soda

Add the tangy taste of lemon to your ginger ale for a special treat.

1 cup ginger ale
Ice cubes
1 teaspoon lemon juice

Lemon slice, for
garnish

Pour the ginger ale over ice in a tall glass. Stir the juice into the ginger ale and garnish with a slice of lemon.

Serves 1

Variations: For a Ginger-Lime Soda, substitute 1 teaspoon lime juice for the lemon juice and proceed as directed above. Garnish with a slice of lime.

For a Ginger-Orange Soda, substitute 1 tablespoon orange juice for the lemon juice and proceed as directed above. Garnish with a slice of orange.

Vanilla Soda

If you love the great taste of vanilla, you will really enjoy this drink.

2 tablespoons vanilla
  syrup
Ice cubes
1 cup carbonated water

2 tablespoons half-and-
  half (optional)
Whipped cream
  (optional)

Pour the syrup over ice in a tall glass. Add the carbonated water and top with the half-and-half and/or whipped cream, if desired.

28
•

Serves 1

Variations: For a Hazelnut Soda, substitute 2 tablespoons hazelnut syrup for the vanilla syrup and proceed as directed above.

For an Almond Soda, substitute 2 tablespoons almond syrup for the vanilla syrup and proceed as directed above.

Vanilla Cola

The vanilla adds a special touch to this cola drink. (Feel free to substitute almond or hazelnut syrup for the vanilla syrup in this drink.)

1 cup cola
Ice cubes

2 tablespoons vanilla
syrup

Pour the cola over ice in a tall glass. Stir the syrup into the cola.

Serves 1

Variations: For a Cherry Cola, substitute 2 tablespoons cherry syrup for the vanilla syrup and proceed as directed above.

For a Chocolate Cola, substitute 2 tablespoons chocolate syrup for the vanilla syrup and proceed as directed above.

For a Lemon Cola, substitute 1 teaspoon lemon juice for the vanilla syrup and proceed as directed above.

Grenadine Cola

The lemon and orange slices give a punchy quality to this cherry cola.

1 cup cola
Ice cubes
1 teaspoon grenadine

Lemon slice, orange
slice, and/or
maraschino cherry,
for garnish

Pour the cola over ice in a tall glass. Stir the grenadine into the cola and garnish with a lemon slice, orange slice, and/or maraschino cherry.

Serves 1

Variation: For a Grenadine Ginger Ale, substitute 1 cup ginger ale for the cola and proceed as directed above.

Cola au Lait

The milk adds a rich taste to the cola.

¾ cup cola
Ice cubes

¼ cup milk

Pour the cola over ice in a tall glass. Stir the milk into the cola.

Serves 1

Cherry Cream Soda

The cherry and vanilla tastes in this drink combine to create a refreshing treat.

¾ cup cream soda
Ice cubes
¼ cup unsweetened
cherry juice

Lemon slice, for
garnish (optional)

Pour the soda over ice in a tall glass. Stir the juice into the soda and garnish with a slice of lemon, if desired.

Serves 1

Root Beer Float

A classic, plain and simple.

¾ cup root beer, chilled
1 scoop vanilla ice
cream

Whipped cream
(optional)

Pour the root beer over the ice cream in a glass. Top with whipped cream, if desired.

Serves 1

Variation: For a Cola Float, substitute ¾ cup cola for the root beer and proceed as directed above.

Chocolate Float

Feel free to use other flavored syrups with this drink (e.g., vanilla, cherry, strawberry), depending on your taste.

2 tablespoons chocolate syrup
1 cup carbonated water, chilled

1 scoop vanilla or chocolate ice cream

Stir the syrup into the carbonated water in a glass. Add the ice cream.

Serves 1

Strawberry Ice Cream Soda

With this drink, the ice cream melts into the milk and provides a strawberry taste.

½ cup milk, chilled
¼ cup carbonated water, chilled
1 scoop strawberry ice cream

Fresh sliced strawberries, for garnish

Pour the milk into a glass. Add the carbonated water and the ice cream and garnish with slices of fresh strawberries.

Serves 1

Variation: For an Orange Sherbet Soda, substitute 1 scoop orange sherbet for the strawberry ice cream and proceed as directed above. Garnish with a slice of orange.

Cherry–Vanilla Ice Cream Soda

This delicious soda is a dessert in itself!

³⁄₄ cup cherry soda, chilled
1 scoop vanilla ice cream

Whipped cream (optional)
Fresh cherry, for garnish (optional)

Pour the soda over the ice cream in a glass. Top with whipped cream and a fresh cherry, if desired.

Serves 1

Variations: For a Cherry–Coffee Ice Cream Soda, substitute 1 scoop coffee ice cream for the vanilla ice cream and proceed as directed above.

For a Cherry–Orange Sherbet Soda, substitute 1 scoop orange sherbet for the vanilla ice cream and proceed as directed above.

PUNCHES

Apple Punch

The great tastes of apple, orange, grape, and strawberry combine in this drink to create a great punch.

2 cups apple juice	Ice cubes
½ cup orange juice	Fresh sliced
½ cup grape juice	strawberries, for
2 cups carbonated water	garnish

Mix the juices and the carbonated water together and pour over ice in 4 tall glasses. Garnish with slices of fresh strawberries.

Serves 4

Variation: For a Grape Punch, substitute 2 cups grape juice for the apple juice and ½ cup apple juice for the grape juice and proceed as directed above.

Apricot Punch

The apricot, orange, and ginger tastes blend together beautifully in this punch.

> 2 cups apricot nectar
> 1 cup orange juice
> 2 cups ginger ale
>
> Ice cubes
> Orange and lemon
> slices, for garnish

Mix the nectar, juice, and ginger ale together and pour over ice in 4 tall glasses. Garnish with slices of orange and lemon.

Serves 4

Orange-Grapefruit Punch

Citrus! Citrus! Citrus!

2 cups orange juice
2 cups grapefruit juice
2 cups carbonated water
  Ice cubes

Orange and
grapefruit slices, for
garnish

Mix the juices and the carbonated water together and pour over ice in 6 tall glasses. Garnish with slices of orange and grapefruit.

Serves 6

Orange-Lemon Punch

This punch combines two of our favorite fruits with one of our favorite sodas — a real treat!

4 cups ginger ale	*Ice cubes*
2 cups orange juice	*Orange and lemon*
2 teaspoons lemon juice	*slices, for garnish*

Mix the ginger ale and the juices together and pour over ice in 6 tall glasses. Garnish with slices of orange and lemon.

Serves 6

41
•

Pineapple-Orange Punch

This tasty, light punch will really quench your thirst.

1 cup pineapple juice	*Ice cubes*
1 cup orange juice	*Pineapple and orange*
2 cups carbonated water	*slices, for garnish*

Mix the juices and the carbonated water together and pour over ice in 4 tall glasses. Garnish with slices of pineapple and orange.

Serves 4

Variation: For a Pineapple-Grape Punch, substitute 1 cup grape juice for the orange juice and proceed as directed above.

Pineapple-Cherry Punch

The pineapple and cherry juices taste great together, and the lemon slices add just the right touch to this drink.

2 cups pineapple juice	Ice cubes
1 cup cherry juice	Lemon slices, for
1 cup carbonated water	garnish

Mix the juices and the carbonated water together and pour over ice in 4 tall glasses. Garnish with slices of lemon.

Serves 4

Pineapple-Mint Punch

This minty refresher makes you feel as if you are on a Caribbean island.

3 cups ginger ale	Ice cubes
1 cup pineapple juice	Fresh mint sprigs, for
1/4 teaspoon mint extract	garnish

Mix the ginger ale, juice, and mint extract together and pour over ice in 4 tall glasses. Garnish with fresh mint sprigs.

Serves 4

Pear–Pineapple Punch

The mandarin orange segments in this drink are a special treat.

    2 cups pear nectar   *Mandarin orange*
    2 cups pineapple juice   *segments, for garnish*
    Ice cubes

Mix the nectar and the juice together and pour over ice in 4 tall glasses. Garnish with segments of mandarin orange.

Serves 4

Pear-Almond Punch

Whether you use the pear or apricot nectar, the almond syrup adds just the right accent to this drink.

4 cups pear nectar
½ cup almond syrup
   Ice cubes

Lemon slices, for garnish

Mix the nectar and the syrup together and pour over ice in 4 tall glasses. Garnish with slices of lemon.

Serves 4

Variation: For an Apricot-Almond Punch, substitute 4 cups apricot nectar for the pear nectar and proceed as directed above. Garnish with slices of orange.

Strawberry-Orange Punch

This punch is great for a summer picnic.

4 cups strawberry
   nectar
2 cups orange juice
   Ice cubes

Strawberry and
orange slices, for
garnish

Mix the nectar and the juice together and pour over ice in 6 tall glasses. Garnish with slices of strawberry and orange.

Serves 6

Variation: For a Strawberry-Grape Punch, substitute 2 cups grape juice for the orange juice and proceed as directed above.

Lemon‑Apple Punch

The lemonade and the apple juice give the ginger ale a special tang in this drink.

1 cup lemonade
1 cup apple juice
2 cups ginger ale

Ice cubes
Fresh raspberries, for garnish

Mix the lemonade, juice, and ginger ale together and pour over ice in 4 tall glasses. Garnish with fresh raspberries.

Serves 4

Kiwi-Apple Punch

The great tastes of kiwifruit and apple mix together perfectly in this punch.

½ cup kiwi syrup
1 cup apple juice
3 cups carbonated water

Ice cubes
Apple and kiwifruit
slices, for garnish

Mix the syrup, juice, and carbonated water together and pour over ice in 4 tall glasses. Garnish with slices of apple and kiwifruit.

Serves 4

Variation: For a Raspberry-Apple Punch, substitute ½ cup raspberry syrup for the kiwi syrup and proceed as directed above. Garnish with fresh raspberries and slices of apple.

Peach-Papaya-Pineapple Punch

The strawberries in this drink provide the perfect garnish.

1 cup peach nectar	*Ice cubes*
1 cup papaya nectar	*Fresh sliced*
1 cup pineapple juice	*strawberries, for*
3 cups carbonated water	*garnish*

Mix the nectars, juice, and carbonated water together and pour over ice in 6 tall glasses. Garnish with slices of fresh strawberries.

Serves 6

Variation: For a Peach-Papaya-Mango Punch, substitute 1 cup mango nectar for the pineapple juice and proceed as directed above.

Pear-Apple-Grape Punch

The apple, grape, and orange tastes complement the pear taste beautifully in this drink.

2 cups pear nectar	Ice cubes
1 cup apple juice	Orange slices, for
1 cup grape juice	garnish

Mix the nectar and the juices together and pour over ice in 4 tall glasses. Garnish with slices of orange.

Serves 4

Mixed Fruit Punch

This refreshing punch combines the great tastes of four of our favorite fruits.

1 cup lemonade	Ice cubes
1 cup orange juice	Orange and
1 cup pineapple juice	grapefruit slices, for
1 cup grapefruit juice	garnish

Mix the lemonade and juices together and pour over ice in 4 tall glasses. Garnish with slices of orange and grapefruit.

Serves 4

Tropical Fruit Punch

Try a taste of the tropics with this punch.

2 cups pineapple juice	Ice cubes
1 cup orange juice	Orange slices, for
½ cup cream of coconut	garnish
2 cups carbonated water	

Mix the juices, cream of coconut, and carbonated water together and pour over ice in 4 tall glasses. Garnish with slices of orange.

Serves 4

SMOOTHIES

Peach Smoothie

This drink is like a peach milkshake — great for a dessert.

1 cup milk, chilled
1 cup peaches, peeled
   and sliced
1 cup vanilla ice cream

Whipped cream
(optional)
Peach slices, for
garnish (optional)

Mix the milk, peaches, and ice cream in a blender for 15 to 20 seconds, or until smooth. Pour into 2 glasses and top with whipped cream and garnish with slices of fresh peach, if desired.

Serves 2

Variations: For a Strawberry Smoothie, substitute 1 cup strawberries for the peaches and proceed as directed above. Garnish with slices of fresh strawberries, if desired.

For a Blueberry Smoothie, substitute 1 cup blueberries for the peaches and proceed as directed above. Garnish with fresh blueberries, if desired.

Apple Smoothie

Add the taste of apple to your vanilla milkshake with this drink.

½ cup apple juice   *¾ cup vanilla ice cream*

Mix both ingredients in a blender for 15 to 20 seconds, or until smooth. Pour into a glass.

Serves 1

Variation: For a Grape Smoothie, substitute ½ cup grape juice for the apple juice and proceed as directed above.

Orange Smoothie

This drink is sure to cool you down on a hot day.

½ cup orange juice   *1 cup vanilla ice cream*

Mix both ingredients in a blender for 15 to 20 seconds, or until smooth. Pour into a glass.

Serves 1

Variation: For a Root Beer Smoothie, substitute ½ cup root beer for the orange juice and proceed as directed above.

Almond Smoothie

Feel free to use chocolate ice cream instead of vanilla ice cream with this drink.

½ cup milk	Whipped cream
¾ cup vanilla ice cream	(optional)
1 tablespoon almond	Sliced almonds, for
syrup	garnish (optional)

Mix the milk, ice cream, and syrup in a blender for 15 to 20 seconds, or until smooth. Pour into a glass and top with whipped cream and sliced almonds, if desired.

Serves 1

Variation: For a Hazelnut Smoothie, substitute 1 tablespoon hazelnut syrup for the almond syrup and proceed as directed above. Garnish with ground hazelnuts, if desired.

Maple Smoothie

It does not get any better than this.

½ cup milk, chilled
¾ cup vanilla or
   chocolate ice cream

1 teaspoon maple syrup

Mix all the ingredients in a blender for 15 to 20 seconds, or until smooth. Pour into a glass.

Serves 1

Peanut Smoothie

This drink is a favorite at juice bars across the country.

½ cup milk
¾ cup vanilla ice cream

2 tablespoons unsalted,
   roasted peanuts

Mix all the ingredients in a blender for 15 to 20 seconds, or until smooth. Pour into a glass.

Serves 1

Variation: For a Chocolate-Peanut Smoothie, add 1 tablespoon chocolate syrup to the ingredients and proceed as directed above.

Apple-Strawberry Smoothie

This elixir is a great pick-me-up.

1 cup apple juice, chilled   *1 cup strawberries,*
                                   frozen

Mix both ingredients in a blender for 15 to 20 seconds, or
until smooth. Pour into 2 glasses.

Serves 2

Pineapple-Blueberry Smoothie

This drink is tart and sweet at the same time.

1 cup pineapple juice, chilled   *1 cup blueberries, frozen*

Mix both ingredients in a blender for 15 to 20 seconds, or until smooth. Pour into 2 glasses.

Serves 2

Variation: For an Orange-Blueberry Smoothie, substitute 1 cup orange juice for the pineapple juice and proceed as directed above.

Strawberry-Banana Smoothie

Whether you use strawberries or pineapple, this drink is a real winner.

1 cup milk, chilled
½ cup strawberries
½ cup banana, peeled
*   and sliced*
1 cup vanilla ice cream

Whipped cream
(optional)
Strawberry and/or
banana slices, for
garnish (optional)

Mix the milk, strawberries, banana, and ice cream in a blender for 15 to 20 seconds, or until smooth. Pour into 2 glasses and top with whipped cream and garnish with slices of fresh strawberry and/or banana, if desired.

Serves 2

Variation: For a Pineapple-Banana Smoothie, substitute ½ cup peeled and sliced pineapple for the strawberries and proceed as directed above. Garnish with slices of fresh pineapple and/or banana, if desired.

Banana-Date Smoothie

This sweet drink makes a great dessert.

2 cups milk
¼ cup banana, peeled
    and sliced
¼ cup dates, pitted
1 cup vanilla ice cream

Whipped cream
(optional)
Banana slices and
pitted dates, for
garnish (optional)

Mix the milk, banana, dates, and ice cream in a blender for 15 to 20 seconds, or until smooth. Pour into 2 glasses and top with whipped cream and garnish with slices of banana and pitted dates, if desired.

Serves 2

Orange-Strawberry-Raspberry Smoothie

Feel free to substitute frozen peaches for the strawberries in this drink.

1 cup orange juice,
   chilled
½ cup strawberries,
   frozen

½ cup raspberries,
   frozen

Mix all the ingredients in a blender for 15 to 20 seconds, or until smooth. Pour into 2 glasses.

Serves 2

Variation: For an Orange-Strawberry-Blueberry Smoothie, substitute ½ cup frozen blueberries for the raspberries and proceed as directed above.

Lemon-Peach-Strawberry Smoothie

Sparkle up your lemonade with this drink.

1 cup lemonade, chilled   *½ cup strawberries,*
½ cup peaches, frozen   *frozen*

Mix all the ingredients in a blender for 15 to 20 seconds, or until smooth. Pour into 2 glasses.

Serves 2

Apple-Blueberry-Banana Smoothie

The blueberries and the banana add a special taste to your apple juice.

1 cup apple juice, chilled *½ cup banana, peeled*
½ cup blueberries, frozen *and sliced*

Mix all the ingredients in a blender for 15 to 20 seconds, or until smooth. Pour into 2 glasses.

Serves 2

Orange-Mango-Banana Smoothie

Add a tropical accent to your orange or pineapple juice with this drink.

2 cups orange juice, chilled

½ cup mango, peeled and sliced

½ cup banana, peeled and sliced

½ cup crushed ice

Mix all the ingredients in a blender for 15 to 20 seconds, or until smooth. Pour into 2 glasses.

Serves 2

Variation: For a Pineapple-Mango-Banana Smoothie, substitute 2 cups chilled pineapple juice for the orange juice and proceed as directed above.

Strawberry-Coconut-Blueberry Smoothie

This red, white, and blue treat is perfect for the Fourth of July.

1 cup milk, chilled
½ cup strawberries, frozen

½ cup blueberries, frozen
¼ cup cream of coconut

Mix all the ingredients in a blender for 15 to 20 seconds, or until smooth. Pour into 2 glasses.

Serves 2

Pineapple-Banana—Orange Sherbet Smoothie

Pretend you are on a tropical island with this drink.

1 cup pineapple juice,
chilled
1 cup banana, peeled
and sliced

$^1/_2$ cup orange sherbet
$^1/_2$ cup crushed ice

Mix all the ingredients in a blender for 15 to 20 seconds, or until smooth. Pour into 2 glasses.

Serves 2

Mixed Berry Smoothie

Berries! Berries! Berries!

$^3/_4$ cup apple juice, chilled
$^1/_4$ cup strawberries,
frozen

$^1/_4$ cup raspberries,
frozen
$^1/_4$ cup blueberries, frozen

Mix all the ingredients in a blender for 15 to 20 seconds, or until smooth. Pour into a glass.

Serves 1

Tropical Fruit Smoothie

Feel free to substitute 1 cup apple juice for the pineapple juice in this drink.

1 cup pineapple juice, chilled
½ cup papaya, peeled and sliced

½ cup strawberries, frozen
2 tablespoons cream of coconut
½ cup crushed ice

Mix all the ingredients in a blender for 15 to 20 seconds, or until smooth. Pour into 2 glasses.

Serves 2

Variation: Substitute ½ cup peeled and sliced banana for the strawberries and proceed as directed above.

SLUSHES

Orange Slush

This treat is fun to drink and easy to make.

½ cup orange juice,   ½ cup crushed ice
* chilled*

Mix both ingredients in a blender for 15 to 20 seconds, or until smooth. Pour into a glass.

Serves 1

Pineapple Slush

This drink is like a low-fat pineapple milkshake.

½ cup milk, chilled　　　　*½ cup crushed ice*
½ cup pineapple, peeled
　and sliced

Mix all the ingredients in a blender for 15 to 20 seconds, or until smooth. Pour into a glass.

Serves 1

Variations: For a Banana Slush, substitute ½ cup peeled and sliced banana for the pineapple and proceed as directed above.

For a Raspberry Slush, substitute ½ cup raspberries for the pineapple and proceed as directed above.

Kiwi Slush

Feel free to try this drink with any of your favorite syrups, or combinations thereof.

¼ cup kiwi syrup   *1 cup crushed ice*
½ cup water, chilled

Mix all the ingredients in a blender for 15 to 20 seconds, or until smooth. Pour into a glass.

Serves 1

Variations: For a Strawberry Slush, substitute ¼ cup strawberry syrup for the kiwi syrup and proceed as directed above.

For a Cherry Slush, substitute ¼ cup cherry syrup for the kiwi syrup and proceed as directed above.

Orange-Pineapple Slush

This drink has a rich, satisfying taste.

*½ cup orange juice,
chilled*

*½ cup pineapple, peeled
and sliced*
½ cup crushed ice

Mix all the ingredients in a blender for 15 to 20 seconds, or until smooth. Pour into a glass.

Serves 1

Variations: For an Orange-Banana Slush, substitute ½ cup peeled and sliced banana for the pineapple. Proceed as directed above.

For an Orange-Peach Slush, substitute ½ cup peeled and sliced peach for the pineapple. Proceed as directed above.

Pineapple-Mango Slush

Pineapple and mango—what a combination!

½ cup milk, chilled
¼ cup pineapple, peeled
*   and sliced*

¼ cup mango, peeled
*   and sliced*
½ cup crushed ice

Mix all the ingredients in a blender for 15 to 20 seconds, or until smooth. Pour into a glass.

Serves 1

Variation: For a Pineapple-Banana Slush, substitute ¼ cup peeled and sliced banana for the mango and proceed as directed above.

Pear-Apple Slush

This treat is perfect for a summer party.

¼ cup pear nectar, chilled	¼ cup apple juice, chilled
	½ cup crushed ice

Mix all the ingredients in a blender for 15 to 20 seconds, or until smooth. Pour into a glass.

Serves 1

Raspberry-Orange Slush

The raspberries add a rich taste to the orange juice in this drink.

¼ cup orange juice, chilled	¼ cup banana, peeled and sliced
¼ cup raspberries	½ cup crushed ice

Mix all the ingredients in a blender for 15 to 20 seconds, or until smooth. Pour into a glass.

Serves 1

Lemon-Strawberry Slush

The tang of the lemonade is tempered by the strawberries in this drink.

½ cup lemonade, chilled　　*½ cup banana, peeled*
½ cup strawberries　　　　　*and sliced*
　　　　　　　　　　　　　　1 cup crushed ice

Mix all the ingredients in a blender for 15 to 20 seconds, or until smooth. Pour into 2 glasses.

Serves 2

Variation: For a Lemon-Raspberry Slush, substitute ½ cup raspberries for the strawberries and proceed as directed above.

Cherry-Papaya Slush

This drink brings the cherry orchard to the tropics.

*¹/₄ cup cherry juice,
    chilled*

*¹/₄ cup papaya, peeled
    and sliced*

*¹/₄ cup banana, peeled
    and sliced*

¹/₂ cup crushed ice

Mix all the ingredients in a blender for 15 to 20 seconds, or until smooth. Pour into a glass.

Serves 1

Coconut-Banana Slush

This white drink is like an ambrosia.

½ cup milk, chilled
2 teaspoons cream of
   coconut

¼ cup banana, peeled
   and sliced
½ cup crushed ice

Mix all the ingredients in a blender for 15 to 20 seconds, or until smooth. Pour into a glass.

Serves 1

Variation: For a Vanilla-Coconut-Banana Slush, add ⅛ teaspoon vanilla extract to the ingredients and proceed as directed above.

Orange-Cantaloupe Slush

The cantaloupe adds a melony taste to the orange juice in this drink.

$\frac{1}{2}$ *cup orange juice,*
chilled

$\frac{1}{2}$ *cup cantaloupe, peeled*
and sliced
$\frac{1}{2}$ *cup crushed ice*

Mix all the ingredients in a blender for 15 to 20 seconds, or until smooth. Pour into a glass.

Serves 1

Vanilla-Hazelnut Slush

This drink is like a milkshake, but without all those calories. Feel free to use other syrups (e.g., strawberry, raspberry, cherry, chocolate) in this drink — either alone or in combinations, depending on your taste.

½ cup milk, chilled
1 tablespoon vanilla
  syrup

1 tablespoon hazelnut
  syrup
¾ cup crushed ice

Mix all the ingredients in a blender for 15 to 20 seconds, or until smooth. Pour into a glass.

Serves 1

Apple-Strawberry-Banana Slush

Three of our favorite fruits blend together in this drink.

½ cup apple juice, chilled
½ cup strawberries
½ cup banana, peeled
  and sliced

½ cup vanilla ice cream
1 cup crushed ice

Mix all the ingredients in a blender for 15 to 20 seconds, or until smooth. Pour into 2 glasses.

Serves 2

Variation: For an Apple-Raspberry-Banana Slush, substitute ½ cup raspberries for the strawberries and proceed as directed above.

Apple-Strawberry-Watermelon Slush

The apple taste mixes perfectly with the strawberry and
the watermelon in this drink.

¼ cup apple juice, chilled
¼ cup strawberries

¼ cup watermelon,
*   peeled, pitted, and*
*   sliced*
½ cup crushed ice

Mix all the ingredients in a blender for 15 to 20 seconds,
or until smooth. Pour into a glass.

Serves 1

Variation: For a Pineapple-Strawberry-Watermelon
Slush, substitute ¼ cup pineapple juice for the apple
juice and proceed as directed above.

Grape-Banana-Papaya Slush

The great taste of grape is complemented by the tropical tastes of banana and papaya in this drink.

½ cup grape juice, chilled

¼ cup banana, peeled and sliced

¼ cup papaya, peeled and sliced

½ cup crushed ice

Mix all the ingredients in a blender for 15 to 20 seconds, or until smooth. Pour into a glass.

Serves 1

Variation: For a Grape-Banana-Strawberry Slush, substitute ¼ cup strawberries for the papaya and proceed as directed above.

Peach-Orange-Banana Slush

The great tastes of peaches, oranges, and bananas mix well in this drink.

½ cup orange juice, chilled

1 cup peaches, peeled and sliced

½ cup banana, peeled and sliced

½ cup orange sherbet

1 cup crushed ice

Mix all the ingredients together in a blender for 15 to 20 seconds, or until smooth. Pour into 2 glasses.

Serves 2

Cranberry-Raspberry-Banana Slush

The raspberries in this drink temper the tartness of the cranberry juice, and the banana and the ice cream add to the sweetness.

½ cup cranberry juice, chilled
½ cup raspberries

½ cup banana, peeled and sliced
1 cup vanilla ice cream
1 cup crushed ice

Mix all the ingredients in a blender for 15 to 20 seconds, or until smooth. Pour into 2 glasses.

Serves 2

Strawberry Yogurt Slush

Feel free to use blueberry yogurt with the strawberries and strawberry yogurt with the blueberries—or either of these fruits or yogurts with the raspberry fruit or yogurt.

1 cup strawberries　　　　*1 cup crushed ice*
½ cup strawberry yogurt

Mix all the ingredients in a blender for 15 to 20 seconds, or until smooth. Pour into a glass.

Serves 1

Variations: For a Blueberry Yogurt Slush, substitute 1 cup blueberries and ½ cup blueberry yogurt for the strawberries and strawberry yogurt and proceed as directed above.

For a Raspberry Yogurt Slush, substitute 1 cup raspberries and ½ cup raspberry yogurt for the strawberries and strawberry yogurt and proceed as directed above.

Banana-Orange-Yogurt Slush

This pick-me-up tastes as good as a milkshake.

*¼ cup orange juice,
  chilled*
*¼ cup banana, peeled
  and sliced*

¼ cup vanilla yogurt
½ cup crushed ice

Mix all the ingredients in a blender for 15 to 20 seconds,
or until smooth. Pour into a glass.

Serves 1

Index

93

Conversion Chart

Equivalent Imperial and Metric Measurements

American cooks use standard containers, the 8-ounce cup and a tablespoon that takes exactly 16 level fillings to fill that cup level. Measuring by cup makes it very difficult to give weight equivalents, as a cup of densely packed butter will weigh considerably more than a cup of flour. The easiest way, therefore, to deal with cup measurements in recipes is to take the amount by volume rather than by weight. Thus, the equation reads:

$$1\,\text{cup} = 240\,\text{ml} = 8\,\text{fl. oz.} \quad \tfrac{1}{2}\,\text{cup} = 120\,\text{ml} = 4\,\text{fl. oz.}$$

It is possible to buy a set of American cup measures in major stores around the world.

In the States, butter is often measured in sticks. One stick is the equivalent of 8 tablespoons. One tablespoon of butter is therefore the equivalent to ½ ounce/15 grams.

Liquid Measures

Fluid ounces	U.S.	Imperial	Milliliters
	1 tsp	1 tsp	5
¼	2 tsp	1 dessertspoon	10
½	1 tbs	1 tbs	14
1	2 tbs	2 tbs	28
2	¼ cup	4 tbs	56
4	½ cup		110
5		¼ pint or 1 gill	140
6	¾ cup		170
8	1 cup		225
9			250, ¼ liter
10	1¼ cups	½ pint	280
12	1½ cups		340
15		¾ pint	420
16	2 cups		450
18	2¼ cups		500, ½ liter
20	2½ cups	1 pint	560
24	3 cups		675
25		1¼ pints	700
27	3½ cups		750
30	3¾ cups	1½ pints	840
32	4 cups or 1 quart		900

Solid Measures

U.S. and Imperial Measures		Metric Measures	
ounces	pounds	grams	kilos
1		28	
2		56	
3½		100	
4	¼	112	
5		140	
6		168	
8	½	225	
9		250	¼
12	¾	340	
16	1	450	
18		500	½
20	1¼	560	
24	1½	675	
27		750	¾
28	1¾	780	
32	2	900	
36	2¼	1000	1
40	2½	1100	
48	3	1350	
54		1500	1½
64	4	1800	
72	4½	2000	2
80	5	2250	2¼
90		2500	2½
100	6	2800	2¾

Conversion Chart

American cooks use standard containers, the 8-ounce cup and a tablespoon that takes exactly 16 level fillings to fill that cup level. Measuring by cup makes it very difficult to give weight equivalents, as a cup of densely packed butter will weigh considerably more than a cup of flour. The easiest way, therefore, to deal with cup measurements in recipes is to take the amount by volume rather than by weight. Thus, the equation reads:

$$1 \text{ cup} = 240 \text{ ml} = 8 \text{ fl. oz.} \quad \tfrac{1}{2} \text{ cup} = 120 \text{ ml} = 4 \text{ fl. oz.}$$

It is possible to buy a set of American cup measures in major stores around the world.

In the States, butter is often measured in sticks. One stick is the equivalent of 8 tablespoons. One tablespoon of butter is therefore the equivalent to ½ ounce/15 grams.

Liquid Measures

Fluid ounces	U.S.	Imperial	Milliliters
	1 tsp	1 tsp	5
¼	2 tsp	1 dessertspoon	10
½	1 tbs	1 tbs	14
1	2 tbs	2 tbs	28
2	¼ cup	4 tbs	56
4	½ cup		110
5		¼ pint or 1 gill	140
6	¾ cup		170
8	1 cup		225
9			250, ¼ liter
10	1¼ cups	½ pint	280
12	1½ cups		340
15		¾ pint	420
16	2 cups		450
18	2¼ cups		500, ½ liter
20	2½ cups	1 pint	560
24	3 cups		675
25		1¼ pints	700
27	3½ cups		750
30	3¾ cups	1½ pints	840
32	4 cups or 1 quart		900

Solid Measures

U.S. and Imperial Measures		Metric Measures	
ounces	pounds	grams	kilos
1		28	
2		56	
3½		100	
4	¼	112	
5		140	
6		168	
8	½	225	
9		250	¼
12	¾	340	
16	1	450	
18		500	½
20	1¼	560	
24	1½	675	
27		750	¾
28	1¾	780	
32	2	900	
36	2¼	1000	1
40	2½	1100	
48	3	1350	
54		1500	1½
64	4	1800	
72	4½	2000	2
80	5	2250	2¼
90		2500	2½
100	6	2800	2¾

ATE